TRANSPORT

Jeff Stanfield

WAYLAND

See for yourself

Homes • School • Shops • The Street • Transport

HOW TO USE THIS BOOK

This book will help you find out all about transport. All the
questions highlighted in **bold** have answers on pages 26–27,
but try to work them out for yourself first. Investigate transport
in your area by trying some of the detective activities on pages
28–29. You'll find difficult words explained on page 30.

Most of the photographs in this book were
taken in Birmingham. So you can compare the
different types of transport in Birmingham
with the transport in your own area.

Series editor: Polly Goodman
Book editor: Mike Hirst
Book designer: Jean Wheeler
Cover design: Dome Design

First published in 1997 by Wayland Publishers Ltd
61 Western Road, Hove, East Sussex BN3 1JD, England

© Copyright 1997 Wayland Publishers Ltd

British Library Cataloguing in Publication Data
Stanfield, Jeff
   Transport. – (See For Yourself)
   1. Transportation – England – Birmingham – Juvenile literature
   2. Transportation – England – Birmingham – Problems, exercises,
   etc. – Juvenile literature
   I. Title
   388'.0942496

ISBN 0 7502 1954 8

Find Wayland on the internet at
http://www.wayland.co.uk

Photographic credits
All the photographs in this book,
except those listed below, were taken
by Angus Blackburn.
Front cover: *bicycle:* Stockfile, *lorry and
racing car:* Tony Stone Worldwide,
motorbike: Pictor. Page 6 (bottom): Robert
Harding Picture Library; page 15 (top) &
25 (bottom): Eye Ubiquitous; page 25 (top):
Sally and Richard Greenhill; pages 4
(bottom), 5 (top), 6 (top), 7 (bottom), 10
(bottom), 16 (top), 17 (bottom), 21 (top), 24,
25 (bottom): Wayland Picture Library.

Typeset by Jean Wheeler, England
Printed and bound in Italy by G. Canale &
C.S.p.A., Turin

CONTENTS

ON THE MOVE

Every day, people are on the move from one place to another. They make all sorts of journeys.

Look at the transport on these pages.

Which vehicles travel on land?

What does the boat travel on?

Have you ever been on any of these vehicles?

▲ This milk float travels on roads.
Many vehicles travel on roads.

Railway trains need special tracks. ▶
They travel on metal rails.

▲ Cars and lorries sometimes drive along motorways.
At this busy motorway junction, the motorway goes
above another road on a flyover.

How do you travel to school?

TWO WHEELS OR FOUR?

◀ Riding a mountain bike is fun. Mountain bikes have lots of gears, which help climb up steep slopes.

The park is a safe place for this boy to ride because there are no cars there.

◀ **Why is he wearing a helmet?**

Some people like riding ▶ motorbikes.

When there is a lot of traffic, motorbikes are good for moving quickly around towns and cities.

6

Cars are the most popular ▶ type of transport.

They help people get from place to place without having to use public transport.

Cars are fast and comfortable, but they are dangerous if people do not drive carefully.

◀ These two girls are wearing safety belts.

What does a safety belt do?

A PLACE TO PARK

Towns and cities have special parking places for cars.

What sign tells ▶ **drivers that they can park here?**

◀ This multi-storey car park has many floors.
Inside, the cars go from floor to floor by driving up and down ramps.

Before the drivers leave the car park, they have to pay for parking their cars here.

Why is it a good idea to build a car park with lots of floors?

Other vehicles need parking places too.

Motorbike riders ▶ can leave their motorbikes at the side of this road.

◀ Cyclists have left their bicycles in this bicycle rack.

How do the cyclists stop thieves from stealing their bicycles?

BUSES AND TAXIS

◀ Small buses like this one make short journeys around town and city centres.

Can you see a sign in the side window?
It tells passengers how much the bus fare costs.

Double-decker buses ▶ are much bigger, so they can carry more passengers.

Every bus travels on a special route.
They go down the same streets, and can stop at the same bus stops on each journey.

10

What does the sign on the front of this bus tell passengers?

▲ A taxi will take you anywhere you want.

A meter inside the taxi shows how much the journey costs.

The further you go, the more money you have to pay.

These taxis are waiting ▶ for passengers.

Why are they waiting outside a shopping centre?

11

COACH TRAVEL

Coaches are like buses, but they are for longer journeys.
They do not stop as often as buses.

▼ This coach is parked in a coach station.
It travels between two big cities.

Can you see which cities the coach travels between?

Where do the passengers put their luggage during the journey?

◀ People often use coach travel when they go out on a day trip.

Have you ever been on a coach trip from your school?

Where is this coach going? ▶

When a coach goes on a long journey, it often has two drivers.

They take turns to drive.

Why does a coach need two drivers for a long journey?

CARRYING CARGO

Transport for goods is just as important as transport for people.

Lorries and vans move large, heavy loads from one place to another.

What are the lorries carrying in the pictures on these pages?

Can you think of some other goods that a lorry might transport?

Articulated lorries are the biggest of all.

The driver sits in the cab at the front.

The cab pulls a long trailer with the cargo inside it.

These two men are ▶ loading an armchair on to a van.

Can you think of a reason why they are moving furniture?

▼ We even need lorries for transporting rubbish.

The rubbish collectors tip the rubbish into the back of the lorry.

Then a machine in the lorry crushes the rubbish to make space.

ON TRACK

◄ Express trains travel between big cities.

They are very fast.

▼ Sprinter trains travel shorter distances. They stop at the smaller stations.

This train takes ► people from the suburbs into the city centre.

Why have these people been into the city?

Main railway stations ▶
in town and city centres
are busy places.

Each platform has
a different number.

◀ A display board tells
people which platform
their train leaves from.
The 08.18 train leaves
from platform 1a.

Where is it going?

These passengers are looking ▶
at a train timetable.
They are finding out what
time their train leaves.

Where do trains go to from your
nearest railway station?

WATERWAYS

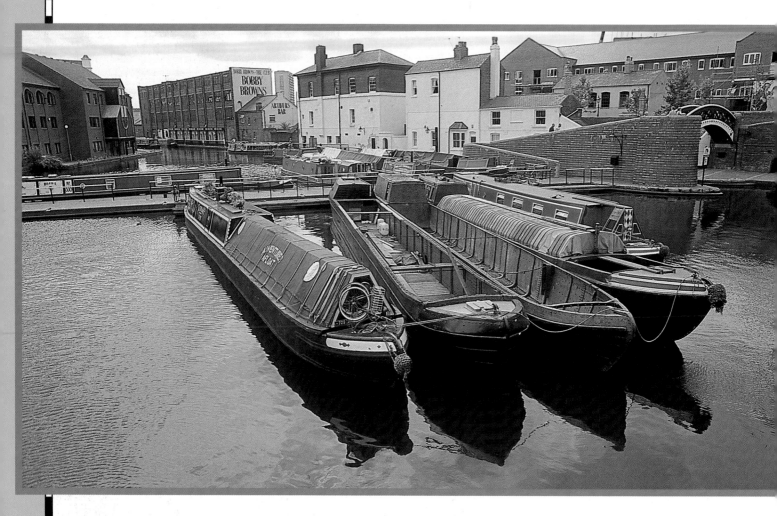

In some places, people use rivers and canals for transport. Before trains and cars were invented, waterways were the best way of transporting cargo around the country.

Goods were loaded into long, narrow boats called barges.

Why are barges this shape?

▲ Barges travel more slowly than trains or lorries. Nowadays, most people make barge journeys for their holidays, or for pleasure trips.
A few people even live on barges.

This barge is ▶ used to help keep the canal banks and bridges in good repair.

Barges are just one type of boat. Can you think of any other kinds?

UP AND AWAY!

Aeroplanes are our fastest type of transport.
They are perfect for going long distances.

Have you ever been on an aeroplane?

Where might you go to on an aeroplane?

Before every flight, ▶ the aeroplane is filled with fuel.

Why do aeroplanes need a lot of fuel?

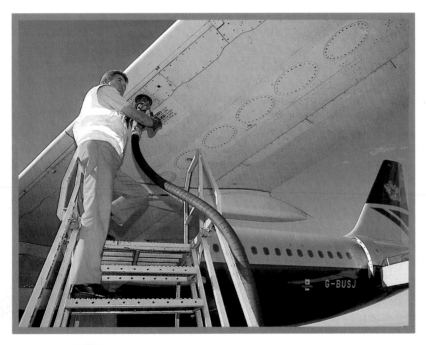

Aeroplanes take off and land at airports.

Before passengers get on an aeroplane, they must show their tickets.

They also hand in luggage to load on to the aeroplane.

Why is this flight ▶
assistant putting
a label on the
woman's suitcase?

◀ You might also see a helicopter at an airport.

Helicopters are smaller than aeroplanes, and they do not need so much space to land or take off.

21

EMERGENCY ALERT

In an emergency, police and firefighters need fast vehicles.

This police motorbike is ▶ rushing to a road accident.

The police car is close behind. ▶

How can you tell that the police car is in a hurry?

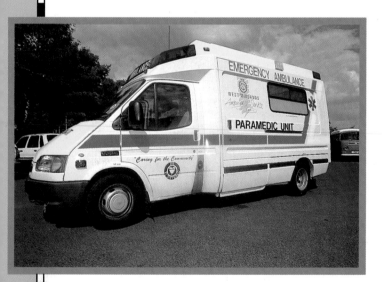

◀ An ambulance is also important in an emergency. If anyone is hurt in the accident, the ambulance will take them quickly to hospital.

Are there any other times when you might need an ambulance?

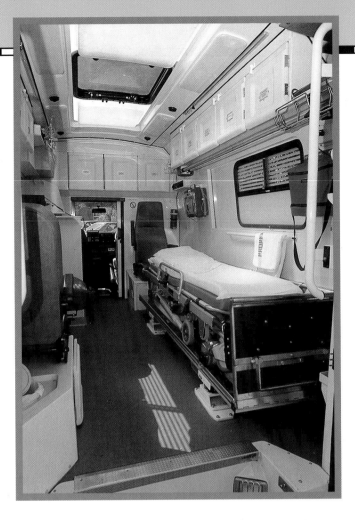

◀ There is a stretcher inside every ambulance to carry injured people.

What else would you find in the ambulance's cupboards?

Firefighters travel to emergencies in a fire engine.

This fire engine ▶ has a strong water cannon on its roof.

The cannon shoots water at fires to put them out.

KEEP MOVING!

If you are disabled, walking can be difficult.

There are special types of transport which help disabled people.

◀ This boy uses a wheelchair to get about.

He is out exploring with a friend.

How can his friend help?

◀ This girl travels to school in a special bus for disabled people.

The bus has a lift at the back.

The lift helps the girl to get on to the bus without leaving her pushchair.

An electric wheelchair ▶ has a motor inside.

The boy twists the handles to make it go. He has to steer the wheelchair, just like a car.

What places would be difficult to get to in a wheelchair?

ANSWERS TO QUESTIONS

Pages 4–5 On the Move

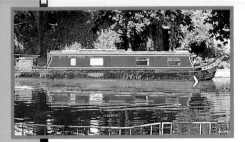

The bicycles, milk float, trains and lorries all travel on land.

The canal boat travels on water.

Pages 6–7 Two Wheels or Four?

The boy is wearing a helmet in case he falls off his bicycle. The helmet will protect his head.

Safety belts keep passengers fastened securely to the car seat, so that if the car stops suddenly or is in an accident, they are not thrown forward and injured.

Pages 8–9 A Place to Park

A white P on a blue background shows a driver where there is a car park.

A car park with lots of floors can fit many cars into a small space.

The cyclists have locked their bicycles to the bicycle rack to keep them safe.

Pages 10–11 Buses and Taxis

The number on the front of the bus tells people which route it will follow. The sign at the front also tells the passengers that the bus is going to a place called West Heath, along the Pershore Road.

The taxis are waiting to take people home from the shops.

Pages 12–13 Coach Travel

The cities are London and Birmingham. Try to find these cities on a map of Britain.

Passengers put their luggage in the hold in the bottom of the coach.

The coach is going to a seaside town called Bournemouth.

On a long journey, a coach driver could become very tired. If there are two drivers, they can take turns to have a rest without stopping the coach.

Pages 14–15 Carrying Cargo

The lorry at the top of page 14 is a tanker carrying oil. Below it is a lorry carrying cars. There is also a furniture van and a rubbish truck.

The men are loading furniture into the van because someone is moving to a new house.

Pages 16–17 On Track

Some of these train passengers have been out shopping in the city centre. Other people might have used the sprinter train for going to work or school, or for visiting friends in another part of the city.

The train on platform 1a is going to Coventry.

Pages 18–19 Waterways

Barges are long and thin to fit in the canals, which are narrow. Most canals were built in the days before big digging machines were invented. Digging long canals by hand was a difficult job, so the builders made the canals as narrow as possible.

Pages 20–21 Up and Away!

Aeroplanes need lots of fuel because they travel for such long distances. The biggest aeroplanes can go for thousands of kilometres without stopping to pick up more fuel.

The label on the woman's suitcase has her name and where she is going on it, so that if the suitcase gets lost, people will know who it belongs to.

Pages 22–23 Emergency Alert

You can tell that the police car is in a hurry because its blue light is flashing. Other traffic should let emergency vehicles pass if their lights are flashing.

The ambulance contains a lot of first-aid equipment. This includes medicines, bandages and an oxygen tank in case anyone has trouble breathing.

Pages 24–25 Keep Moving!

The boy's friend can help him go faster by pushing the wheelchair. The boy can also move it himself by pushing the wheels with his hands.

DETECTIVE ACTIVITIES

Finding out about transport is lots of fun. You can become a transport detective and learn about the kinds of transport near your home. Always ask an adult to help you if you are doing detective work outdoors. Be especially careful near roads or railway lines.

● Look in old magazines for pictures of different kinds of transport. Cut them out and sort them into different types, such as boats, aircraft, cars and lorries. Stick them on to a big sheet of paper in sets.

● Keep a transport record of the different vehicles you see near your home. How many different kinds can you see during one weekend?

● What is your favourite journey? It might be a walk, a car ride, or a bicycle ride. Draw a picture map to describe it.

● What should you wear to be a really safe cyclist? Make a list, or draw a picture of a safe cycling outfit.

● Roads have lots of signs to tell drivers what to do. Next time you go out in a bus or a car, draw some of the signs you see. When you get home, ask an adult what they mean. You might have to check some signs in a book called *The Highway Code*.

● Travel tickets come in all sorts of shapes and sizes. Make a collection of tickets. For example, they can be bus tickets, train tickets or parking tickets. Use them to make a collage picture.

● If you visit a motorway service station, make a list of the different things you see there. Draw a picture map of the service station to show the different activities.

• Collect the route numbers of buses in your local area. Look at the display board at the front or on the sides of the bus. Write down the place that each route goes to.

• With some friends, make up a play about a bus journey. One person should be the driver, and the others can be passengers.

• Using old boxes, make a model of a train. Decide whether it will be a big express train or a local sprinter. Once you have finished the train, you could also make a model station.

• Lorry spotting is fun! Make a list of the different kinds of lorry you see in your area. If you can, write down what each lorry is carrying.

• Visit your local fire station when it has an open day. Look at the fire engines. What can you see inside them, to help the firefighters in an emergency?

• Draw a picture of a fire engine and firefighters putting out a fire.

• This book shows you photographs of canal boats. What other types of boat can you think of? Draw pictures of them on a big sheet of paper, and make a boat poster. Don't forget that boats travel on other kinds of water besides canals.

• Make up a play about going abroad on holiday. Where will you go? How will you get there? If you go on an aeroplane, what will you do when you get to the airport?

• Find out about your nearest airport. Where do the aeroplanes fly to? Use a world atlas to find out where these places are.

• People who use wheelchairs find some places difficult to get to. Think about the journey from your home to the nearest shops. Would it be easy to make this journey in a wheelchair? Draw a picture map of the journey, and show any problems on the map.

• Make up an A–Z alphabet book of transport. Think of a transport word and draw a picture for each letter of the alphabet.

DIFFICULT WORDS

Articulated lorries Lorries that have two separate parts: a cab and a trailer.

Barges Boats that travel on rivers and canals. Most barges carry cargo.

Cargo The things that are carried by a lorry, ship or aeroplane.

Double-decker buses Buses with two floors.

Express trains Fast trains.

Flyover A bridge carrying one road or railway over another.

Gears Gears help vehicles to go faster, and to climb up steep slopes.

Helmet A hard hat that protects people's heads.

Motorway A big road, with two or three lanes of traffic going each way. Only cars and lorries can travel on a motorway.

Multi-storey car park A car park with several different floors.

Passengers People who are travelling in a vehicle.

Route When a vehicle goes the same way many times, it goes on the same route.

Safety belts Belts that fasten people safely into their seats while they travel.

Sprinter trains Trains that make short journeys and stop at smaller stations.

Suburbs The outer parts of a town or city. Suburbs have lots of houses and flats for people to live in.

Traffic All the different vehicles that come and go in a street or a town.

Vehicles Machines for transporting people or things. Cars, trains and boats are all vehicles.

Other Books to Read

Flight Attendant by Alison Cooper and Diana Bentley (Wayland, 1990)

Journeys by Helen Barden (Wayland, 1992)

Maps and Journeys by Kate Petty (A&C Black, 1993)

Mapwork 1 by David Flint and Mandy Suhr (Wayland, 1992)

Mapwork 2 by Julie Warne and Mandy Suhr (Wayland, 1992)

On the Move by Ruth Thomson (Watts Books, 1993)

A River Journey by Paul Humphrey and Alex Ramsay (Evans, 1994)

Train Driver by Alison Cooper and Diana Bentley (Wayland, 1990)

Transport Around the World by Godfrey Hall (Wayland, 1995)

INDEX

Page numbers in **bold** show that there is a photograph as well as information on that page.